the debt

the debt

POEMS

ANDREAE CALLANAN

BIBLIOASIS
WINDSOR, ON

FIRST EDITION

Library and Archives Canada Cataloguing in Publication

Title: The debt : poems / Andreae Callanan.
Names: Callanan, Andreae, 1977- author.
Description: Poems.
Identifiers: Canadiana (print) 20210122528 | Canadiana (ebook) 20210122587 | ISBN 9781771964173
(softcover) | ISBN 9781771964180 (ebook)
Classification: LCC PS8605.A45 D43 2021 | DDC C811/.6—dc23

Edited by Luke Hathaway
Copyedited by Emily Donaldson
Cover and interior illustration: "Water Carrier I" by Diana Daly. Used by permission of the artist.
Text and cover designed by Christina Angeli

Published with the generous assistance of the Canada Council for the Arts, which last year invested $153 million to bring the arts to Canadians throughout the country, and the financial support of the Government of Canada. Biblioasis also acknowledges the support of the Ontario Arts Council (OAC), an agency of the Government of Ontario, which last year funded 1,709 individual artists and 1,078 organizations in 204 communities across Ontario, for a total of $52.1 million, and the contribution of the Government of Ontario through the Ontario Book Publishing Tax Credit and Ontario Creates.

PRINTED AND BOUND IN CANADA

FOR SUSIE

Contents

the debt

Promise

These are the rumours: rapturous
clash of sea-stones heaving
under the chill collapse
and pull of tide to shore, moss
padding the shaded forest
floor in deepest green shot
through with chartreuse
strands, the marshes inlaid
with autumn fruit. Time-carved
cathedrals of cliff,
congregations of gannets.
How many colours
pulse in a single shard
of Labrador feldspar? What
is the sound of twenty thousand
seabirds calling through silken
fog?

Promise me it isn't all just wild
and wave-wracked
promise.

Crown

> [We grant our trusty and wellbeloved servant … free liberty and license …] to discover, search, find out and view such remote, heathen, and barbarous lands, countries, and territories [as are] not actually possessed by any Christian prince or people.
>
> —Queen Elizabeth I, *Charter to Sir Walter Raleigh: 1584*, as read by Prince Charles to an assembled crowd in St. John's, Newfoundland, 1983

What he meant was *uncultured*. What he meant
was *bestial*. What he meant was *far-flung*,
yes, but also *improbable*, as though
this place were mere outside chance. When the Crown
came, it came with baubles, with dancers, no
end to the gifts and tokens shared among
the fuss-hungry masses. The Crown was bent
on shoring up our love of monarchy.
At the bedrock edge of the Atlantic,
the Crown saw ocean possessed by no one.
The Crown claimed it. Sometimes a ship goes down
and takes all hands; a man cannot outgun
an ocean. The Crown remembers frantic
spadework, the rush to plant a colony.

Planted in our little colony, we kept ourselves useful by keeping busy. Out of sight. Those were years of a quiet harbour, the White Fleet long gone and its dockside soccer matches long over, *Tchau, Novos Mares!* We were used-book shoplifters, record-store hangers-on in torn jeans and scuffed Army-Navy boots. War Memorial loiterers, Sharpie graffiti artists defacing the white chipped stone of the national monument, reasoning that the war dead, spared their gruesome end, would have done the same. The King and Country that they died for were not our king, not our country. We were outpost, not empire, nothing but a pack of heathen city kids.

Pack of city kids: we couldn't have known
what *no more codfish* meant. We would never
have made it as fishermen anyway:
our world was girders and concrete. No boats.
Our parents hadn't raised us in this grey
maze of roads to go on the water. Clever—
or, we thought we were—whooping at the phone-
in radio callers, their voices rough
from salt air and cigarettes and inhaled
affirmatives. Men who'd always hauled nets.
Women who'd split a million fish, their throats
raw from plant-floor cold. And we would place bets,
choke back laughs as the bravest prankster dialled,
no sense to know when enough was enough.

Enough is never enough when the TV tells you there's another world out there, speaks to you in flattened English, makes you want to flatten yourself into an envelope and mail yourself to Toronto so you can dance yourself sick on *Electric Circus*. I spent half my life in front of MuchMusic, a blank tape in the VCR in case a veejay read a request from Newfoundland. I didn't even care that they couldn't say "Newfoundland." One time, a St. John's band dropped by the studios at 299-Queen-Street-West-Toronto-Ontario to sing a song for the cameras. It was Christmas, and they sang about home: *John Crosbie, one brainstormy night / had a vision, how to set the wrong right. / "It's seasonal work, don't you see, / we'll take all those men of the sea, / make them all clauses, / mister and missus / there won't always be fishes, / but there will always be wishes...."* I sat on my floor and whispered, *don't tell them that, guys. You're giving away too much.*

I've said too much already. I had sworn
I wouldn't breathe a word about the stand
of golden raspberries behind the school,
or mention the apple tree spiralling low
with bright fists of fruit. A grandfather's rule:
take some, leave some, tell no one. You understand,
it's born of fear of empty pantries, born
of a hungry history. It makes martyrs
of us all come fall, wasp stings and heatstroke,
panic-picking to fill each cellar shelf.
But it feels wrong that I should know
an apple tree, keep a berry patch to myself.
Come here, I'll draw you a map. If he woke,
my grandfather'd have my guts for garters.

I'll have your guts for garters, I'll crown ya, I'll cuff ya, get in off the jesus road, put your goddamn bike in the yard, your dinner's cold now, it's ruint. It was a tough-love street, and I was a bookish kid, and the infill houses where I babysat had empty cupboards save for packs of noodles and those marshmallow cookies shaped like four-petalled flowers, checkered pink and white, a biscuit base and coconut all over, the most pastel food I could imagine. I could scramble eggs, I could bake fishsticks. I could put the kids to bed without reading (nothing to read) and wander downstairs into the finished basement ashtray pornmag rec room. But only once. I was raised in a house with no men. This was not my world, not my time, the grit of it someone else's industry.

The sediment of another era's
industry (the flour mill, the tannery)
slows the river to a drunkard's pace: around
the tennis complex, past the stadium,
it heaves itself toward the lake. Brown trout
still draw anglers in rubber livery,
despite reports of fish kill. Now, dare us
to scrabble down the bank in canvas shoes,
muddying our white socks as we
bunch fragrant wild mint, piling up armloads
of toothed green leaves: we'll do it. Radiant
pageant queens with weedy bouquets bestowed
on us by a last-century city.
This is childhood. We live it how we choose.

We lived our childhoods how we chose, half feral half the time, acting the young sophisticates the other half, local intellectual royalty talking politics until sunrise in the all-night coffee and doughnut shop. Proper diplomats. At sixteen I started renting foreign films from the corner video shop and watching them alone: *Godzilla vs. Mothra* one week, *The Seventh Seal* the next. *Nosferatu. Roman Holiday.* I was indiscriminate in my longing for new tongues, new scenery. Baby cinephile, baby critic. I devoured subtitles, dreamt of passports, plane tickets, an apartment and a video-store membership in my very own name.

We take care of the things that bear our names.
We take care of our houses, cheques. Our children.
The rest is someone else's business. What
falls outside the fence line—beyond the rock
walls, silvering softwood posts, the slipknot-
secured gates—that's called *Crown land*. The heathen
without a heath knows a peculiar shame:
the empire sends scraps, and so our scraps
to the empire we return. We bank trails
with refrigerators, washers, dryers,
rolls of carpet. Leave burnt-out cars to block
paths, toss blasty boughs on tire fires.
Berries blaze through ragged, rusting coils
of mattresses resigned to slow collapse.

At times it seemed that everyone was resigned to slow collapse, the way the garbage collected under the patches of cow parsnip and Queen Anne's lace, the way the empty storefronts blinked their blackened eyes at you when you walked by. We killed time at Harbourside, standing in a ring, staring at each other's feet until someone came along with something to kick. One summer, we spent our nights in a field between my two best friends' houses, plotting capers. Overnight in the graveyard. Overnight at the park. Overnight on a bridge. Overnight wandering east-end suburbs, thinking these outings wild and daring exploits.

Outside, we tend our wild and weedy things,
leave makeshift gardens behind each time
we pack up for another midnight move.
We don't invest. No-one tells us our plants
were brought here from afar, the empire's proof
of conquest: an old conservatory crime
of specimens turned backyard escapees.
Good morning to catsfoot's evergreen paws.
Hello, jewel-like blossoms of touch-me-not,
nodding above stems that gleam translucent.
Hello to mile-a-minute's swift advance.
The black soil behind our new apartment—
all apartments—is lead-laced and noxious.
Our weeds don't care; they've long since naturalized.

My friends and I naturalized, made ourselves at home in every parent's living room. We were good kids. We would go far. We wanted to go far away and never look back, wrap Newfoundland in old newspaper and hide it under our beds. Maybe dust it off and wear it like a comic tiara at parties, sport it at an angle, *it's on squish, your crown's on squish*. In Canada, I softened my hard *R*s when I spoke, lowered my gaze each time I passed a billboard begging me to save the beleaguered seals: blood crystallizing on pack ice, big-eyed bedlamers snapped immobile. *You don't do that, do you? No, say it in your accent! What do you mean you can't finish your drink—I thought you were from Newfoundland. Hang on, I have a joke to tell you.* I learned their jokes, told them myself so I wouldn't have to hear them, my tiara on squish, glinting gold.

But in the spring, such abundance of gold
bursting from grim cracks in city sidewalks,
nodding *yes, throw your jacket down and sit*
small and joyous on the sun-warmed concrete.
Raw material for a coronet
fit for an urchin in a tinderbox
town. Milky stems stain my skirt where I hold
my pulled flowers, stamp a constellation
of gasping *O*s that will never wash out.
I slit with my bitten-down nails these same
stems, slide one through the next till I complete
a chain, a circle. A crown: flimsy frame
on untamed hair, yellow pollen fallout.
Sticky, bitter fingertips. My station.

The water-carriers

after the photograph *Two women, four buckets* by Edith S. Watson, c. 1900

From a distance, you might think the girls
are wearing farthingales, crinolines.
Pairs of sinewy arms and weighted pails
braced at hip-height by wooden water-hoops
trick the eyes into seeing sweeping skirts
fit for plantation-owners' daughters.

Your mind might make a palimpsest,
sketch slender ribs of steel, crosshatch
horsehair over each bent-birch apparatus,
wrap entire girls in satin and send
them off to the dance, callused hands
unclenched and gloved in kidskin, wrists
wrapped in sapphire circlets, in silver, palms
open and idle.

Don't credit their slenderness to whalebone
and lacing; put it down to heavy lifting,
a lifetime of letting the men eat first.

Barrens

> After the frost, the "marshes and barrens" afford miles of colour.
>
> —Victoria Hayward, *Romantic Canada*, 1922

After the frost, miles
of colour: wild red
and black currants,
rowan berries,
bakeapples. Partridge-
berries like garnet beads,
blueberries bunched
like dusted clusters of
moonstone, low against
cracks and scarpings of cliffs
where one would not
suppose a thimbleful
of earth could cling.

Vocabulary

The year I was born, so
was the compound *strip mall.*
I am matched by *hydrochlorofluorocarbon*
for turns around the sun: same
for *biodefense, ecotoxicology,*
and *deconstructionism.*
When I shouldered my way
into the world, I came with
exercise bike and *kitesurfing, heptathlon*
and *jumper's knee. Text message,*
upload, download, and I
could have shared a nursery.
Warp speed, power chord,
radar gun.

The year I was born,
white-bread proclaimed itself
adjective, *guilt-trip* turned
verb, and *plus-one* added
itself to the nouns.
Point person nudged out
point man. Beam weapon,
brownfield. Expert system.
Knowledge engineering.

An anxious age, a year
of too much: *gazillion,*

megahit, *supercentre*. I have
no longing for such excess.
Leave me with the quietest
of my cohort: *grapholect*, *geometrics*.
Earth-sheltered.

Entertainer

Our faces were his, but never
our names: our father,

in his rush to plant a colony,
failed to build a fence

at the top of the thirty-foot
cliff that edged his land. Dogs

and ducks and chickens kept
their distance through instinct. We

kept our distance through fear.
We sifted soil year upon year

to grow the carrots straight,
dreamed stones when we closed

our eyes at night. He won over
the crag-faced locals with his crawlspace

homebrew and highway sagas, his country
songs sending them staggering

along fogbound, lightless roads. Always
the entertainer. He'd invented a handle

for the stage, and kept it. Changed
his ID but never altered ours.

Night-waking

Half the time, it's swarming, stinging bees
at your elbows, the backs of knees,

which I blame on the hum of the neighbours' bathroom fan
downstairs, and I make a plan

to ring the landlord first thing and complain.
Now and then it's rain

that washes an ocean into your head,
makes tossing shipwreck splinters of your bed

and a bobbing berg of you,
devours bears and dolls and blankets, too.

The odd time it's spiders, and your eyes fly
open and dart about while I

bend and mime a heroic sweep,
send imagined intruders away to burrow deep

between the floorboards. One night
it was a fox that bit your hand right

off, then slipped out the door and down the hall to hide.
You held your wrist, and cried,

and curled your fingers into a wounded paw,
which I stroked for half an hour to draw

back out into full length.
It was another half hour before your voice's strength

had waned, and your breath had grown slow,
and your sharp sobs turned to quiet. Soft now, low.

Mantel

after the painting *Just an Illusion* by Kym Greeley, 2016

No stacks of books, no fat file-folders
crammed with annotated sheets, ridged
edges a baleen grin. No pencils, no pens.
No stubs of crayons skinned by toddlers'
agile, focused fingers. No rings
of house keys hiding, no angled orphaned
arms of sunglasses long since replaced.
No months-old greeting cards,
no loot bags emptied of all the best loot,
no framed photos, no unframed photos,
no business cards, no packs of matches
grabbed from little hands and deposited
somewhere safe. No tax receipts,
no irate bills shrieking for payment.
No snapped elastics, no strands of silver
bracelets, their lobster-claw clasps
torn clean. No dust. No broken
watches, no broken bits of toys,
no jam-jar-propped weedy wildflowers,
lupins idly pulled while passing, daisies
snatched and brought home roots and all.

None of these. This fireplace mantel
is a white expanse against a wall as pink
as the smooth inside of a souvenir

seashell. Not grand, but grand
enough to recall a time of taking
time to finish work with elegance, a few
carved details here, a measured symmetry
there. Uncluttered, civil, the mantel bears
a single houseplant: a dense-fleshed begonia,
its cordate leaves profuse and shadow-veined,
riotous, thriving in a hunched pot the colour
of rust. Complete, contained.

Carousel at the Christmas market, Brussels

There are no horses here.
Instead, it's gear
and scaffold, machinery
exposed, the stomachbody
of an octopus, legs pooling
on the floor and then unfurling
as the creature rises.
These are all surprises:
the caterpillar, the snail,
the outstretched, pale
wings of the pterodactyl,
bone to bone a bone-white sail.
Count the coils of tin and copper
on the child-sized helicopter,
watch the cello
lean against its own bow,
try to right itself and push
its music out. With a rush
and a metal grind, a spaceship,
let's say rocket, shudders up
and out the top
carrying a wide-eyed astronaut
who touches the glass with one small hand,
waves to the city, to the stars beyond.

Winter

The adults warned my mother
never to eat snow, never
even to catch flakes on her tongue.
Each hexagon in a time of testing
harboured in its symmetry a nuclear threat,
even though her island was half a world away
from those in pictures,
shrinking under their mushroom clouds.

In front of the TV, in the days of TV,
when the one clear channel channels
national news into our living room,
my mother tries to keep ahead of
the weather by building up a stock
of mittens. Practical and almost pretty,
tactical use of bits and scraps. Rough
wool, coarsely spun, means our mitts
soak through with each snowball
we shape, each trench we dig. They slip
from our cold-pinched wrists, stitches caked
with small white bullets, crystals compacted
to something like ice. We chew
at the geodes in our cupped palms,
wool-threaded rock candies laced with road salt.

My mother never heeded fallout
warnings. None of them did.

Fatalists even in childhood, they knew
nothing that fell from the sky as feathered
water could ever be avoided.

She knits with a speed that seems
the stuff of cartoons: heroic, impossible.
But we are young, and our hands
are very small.

My mother's cigarette

Punctuation mark, point-prover.
Satisfier of need. Calmer of rattled
nerves. Shield behind which
shyness quivered. Social pyrotechnic.
Changer of vocal register. My most
important errand: grey bike over railroad
tracks with a note for the shopkeep
granting permission for the nine-year-old
bearer to purchase one pack of Matinée
Extra Mild. No laws
against that, then.

Scarlet satellite, nearly
silent, tracing its elliptical orbit
through the apartment's electric
air.

Impromptu

September, almost, and the man-made pond
is ringed with families trying to rescue
the last few days of a dying summer.
We promised we'd have take-out in the park—
illicit banquet on a weekday night.
I balance my plate, squint at the pyrite
glint of the water. Our kids disembark
from their bench. Blue shadows spread like rumours,
and just beyond some thick clumps of fescue
two young herring gulls—local toughs—abscond

with someone's dinner scraps. We eat faster,
two sets of eyes alert, scanning the stones
that line the pool, watching as our children
scatter along its bank like marbles loosed
shining from an unstitched pocket, colliding,
bounding. They are made of motion, striding
to the edge of earshot. Our cupped hands boost
our calls, bounce them over pools that roughen
into ripples. Our daughter stands alone,
ignores us, pesters swans, courts disaster.

The engineer

Five years old: too young to read,
or wander far alone, or stay in school
for more than half the day. With startling
speed he outgrows boots and jeans.

Sometimes he dedicates himself
to sullenness and temper, the worst
parts of his character. Right now, he steadies
a blocky spacecraft he's put together

from neatly interlocking bricks
and planks, studs and hinges, a tiny
black door-frame, small grey pins. *Watch this,*
Mom, he says, and yanks a cylinder from

the ship's tail. The same thing happens
this and every time: pieces clatter
to the floor, slide, disperse. He watches
as the broken craft releases its minuscule

spaceman, as lasers on the segmented wings
deploy and arc, unguided and unbidden. At first
he stares, then switches gears: mechanics
to forensics. How did it go wrong?

The ejector seat was loaded right. All the base
plates were firmly set. He scans the wreck

of rectangles at his feet and beneath mine,
raw materials for building worlds.

Last week he might have stamped his heel,
and frowned, and if the spirit moved
him, hurled the last bits of his spaceship
to the ground. Today, it's in his nature

to be calm, say *Look, Mom, look,* as he gathers
scattered pieces. *Look, Mom,* as he starts
again. *Watch, Mom.* Miniature astronaut ascends
and plummets.

Golden

My daughter can explain it all:
the biggest hits of nineteen
twenty-nine, each step
from vaudeville to sound stage,
casting and costuming, choreography
for triple threats. The slapdash
scaffolds of a quick-and-dirty
Golden Age.

I can explain none of it:
how this child has outgrown
me, her worn pink shoes now larger
than my own. This child who began
to dance three months before she was born.
I have no explanation for the dancing.

The screen flashes silver
while my daughter corrects
the turns of dancers long since turned
to dust. She breathes her ambition
into the air between us. Under
the fractal branches of a metallic
tree, unnumbered figures swirl
in black and white. They spin
into a sequinned froth
and their *pointe,* I am informed,
is terrible.

Asymmetry

Left elbow broken at the age of three
and never quite corrected, bending rogue,
impeding push-ups, locking
me into a childhood of purple
participation ribbons. Left ankle, thick
from decades of sprains and fractures,
stiff and reluctant and no doubt
a site of arthritis to come. Left
eye, weak, taking in a blur through pop-bottle
glasses lens, its right-side partner compensating,
always overworked, doing its best but leaving
me clumsy and anxious. Left corner
of my mouth, scarred from a winter's
collision with dense, untended branches
at the base of a snow-covered hill,
an evening's sledding brought to a bloody
halt, a lump of lip growing where no lump
should be, a red crack at the edge
of each self-conscious school-photo smile.

The next-to-smallest finger of my left hand,
embedding my ring in its bulging flesh,
a fat tree swallowing a chain-link fence.

To my spine

You've got a lot of nerve.
You've got all the information.
My body's rolling highway, my body's

rising and falling railroad. My body's
cordillera, meaning cord, meaning
little rope. Little knotted rope

gripped by big knotted muscles
in need of kneading back to pliancy.
Gentle curve, gentle arch, gentle

ridge of the softest geometry.
The geometry hills have. Beaches.
Streams. Swaying column, creaking

ladder, sounder of cracks and pops,
you demand wringing-out, wish
to be folded, draped. Where

do you find the resolve to keep
me upright when some days it's all
I can do to keep my head on straight?

Aubade

The radio whispers us awake. We sleep
light, rouse easy. The day is dark still,
new. We are also new, charmed
by the newness of a shared bed,
with sleeping twined like bindweed
sprawling rampant over field and fence,
burying land that's been left fallow.

A room away, my tiny daughter turns
and shifts, summoning creaks from mattress
springs, murmuring into air. We hear
her stir and we play statue, unbreathing
until her faintest sounds subside.

I've kept you from her, fearing
flight, fearing that loss compounded
is worse than loss alone,
that I'll wake to find you disentangled
and gone. But daybreak after daybreak
you are here, and I long to tell you, *stay*,
to call off the daily goodbyes.

My tongue won't move, lies thick
and slow behind my teeth, a slug
curled tight inside a night-closed flower.

We dress; we walk in silence to the door.
You're the lone man in the street, stepping
backwards, first, to keep me with you
longer, then turning, striding off,
collar up against the dawn's damp chill.

Morning presses the full length
of its pale, calm fingers to the harbour's
open mouth. The harbour doesn't
say a thing.

Cement

Here's a thing I wish I'd done, but didn't do:
All week, municipal workers have been
laying new concrete on Bond Street's broken,
green-veined sidewalks. No time to lose: the school
will open soon. The air's been damp and cool.
There's been a fair bit of rain. Cling-
wrap, raised up by safety-orange wooden
horses, protects the soft pavement for a full
city block. I know that it must be bad form
to dream of vandalism, to want
so badly to claim the clean, newpoured,
caresmoothed surface, to need to flaunt
good fortune. But I wish that, between downpours,
I'd run and scrawled my name there, loving yours.

Weatherproof

We hang the storm door and caulk
the cracks, seal the spaces between
the slats to mask the old wood's
warp. Double the windows,
though the winter panes shudder and bay
with each jagged northwesterly.
Call for propane and oil. The snow
will come by flake, by flurry,
by squall and wave and wall,
will bank and drift in layers
against the house. Will dust,
then stick, then bury. Will be
removed and then replaced.
It will come soon and it will
stay long. We brace and gird. Stay
in, stay warm, take our vitamins, drink
our tea. Stare from the kitchen
past steeple and station, at the hills
just beyond, at the white, then grey,
then black spruce green,
then white, then grey again.

ICU

I got used to the other people. The family
whose mother was killed on the highway,
her husband still poorly.
The elderly woman, her grown
children no comfort at night when
the monitor's light cast
orange shadows of snaky tubes,
her shaky voice calling out for anyone,
anyone at all. We'd all done a day
or two together, talking about the weather
and the traffic on the road into town,
speaking the code of not knowing
what to say. *This one's husband*
may not make it. That one's father's
in no good shape, doctor said so. It's
a shame, a shame, a shame. No one told
me their name, what they were doing
before they got the call, ran out the door
and boarded a plane without packing.
We sat, side by side, red eyes
tracking the path of each passing
nurse. Someone pulled mints
from a purse and we breathed cold
breath, in silence, praying, weighing
the odds of our going and staying.

Summer motel

I can't help laughing, having handed all
our money to the woman at the front.
Both of us penniless now, till we haul
ourselves to Gander later. We're buoyant

with the idea of *motel*, thrilled by
the frankness of it, the lack of frill.
Our temporary neighbours' children fly
past, calling like kittiwakes, coarse and shrill,

disturbing the bright surface of the pool.
They perch on broken bits of coloured foam,
fling water at each other. A small, cruel
colony of cousins, friends while they're away from home.

We look like tourists playing honeymoon.
The swimmers eye us, hope we're leaving soon.

House sparrow

Little message, tiny
feathered communiqué: how did you
find your way in between my window's
antiquated panes? Pressed
like a living picture, just able
to turn your body around. You jerk,
timorous and wild, head cocked,
black eye blinking, alarmed
as the loose glass rattles when I
gingerly lower the time-worn
frame. I work against gravity,
fraction of an inch after fraction
of an inch. Because which is worse
luck: a bird in the house, or killing
that bird while trying to free it?
Fraction of an inch, fraction of an inch,
and you finally hop up, take flight,
light on the kitchen shelf, inspect
my houseplants, catch your breath.
I raise the window to its full height,
scatter sunflower seeds on the sill
to try to lure you out. So what
does it mean when you circle
the room, then fly to the window,
and fall between the trembling panes
again?

Vacant lot

All summer, the children recited
the names of the diesel creatures
that lurched and roared at the top
of our street: excavator, front-end
loader, bulldozer, dump truck. Empty
space turned to storage for gravel
and lengths of PVC. Rumours
of new infrastructure, something to fill
the gap where the hospital had been.

A summer of dust stirred up,
of mammoth machines belching
black grit, of nine-to-five digging
and dumping. A thrill for three
little ones, a trial for a nervous
mother who heard shrieking brakes,
hydraulic gasps when she went to sleep
each night.

And then it was gone, nothing
but a flat plane of chipped stone behind
the galvanized fence. We grew out of trucks,
and the lot grew into a meadow. I recite
the names of flowers: clover, daisies,
vetch, burdock, curled dock, evening
primrose. Mugwort, thistles, goldenrod,
wild mustard.

Putting up

Call it canner's greed: smug with pride
at my new-learned skill of trapping

fall's free bounty in federally approved
glass, I wage war on the birds who

panic their way toward winter. They
have begun their occupation of our yard.

I shoo starlings, startle waxwings. I pick
blackcurrants, and, when my baskets are full,

I toss the fruit into the waiting pot, flick
with my purpled thumbnail a hundred

new-hatched snails into the sink. On
the hob, the currants pop and splutter,

paint blue bruises up my forearms, smear
violent streaks on the off-white stovetop. After

I've heaved a crock from the cupboard to
catch the dripping juice, I watch the jelly bag

hang dense and heavy. It's a picture fit for a
butcher shop, as though the stained muslin

strains against something used to beating,
turning cold.

Fall fiscal update, with damsons

I know
that all
signs
point to
have-not,

but I've
got more
plums
than can
fit in
my
jam pot.

Exhibit

Gannets perched up top, stately, still.
Carved polystyrene crags, coastline
grasses massed and paint-spattered

to look for all the world like shit-matted
nests. Eggs everywhere, some tucked
around the stationary feet of razorbills

and turr, some untended and conspicuous.
Smashed shells, smashed whelk, smashed urchin,
upturned hollow carapace of crab. Dirty

shafts of fallen feathers, spare, barbless.
Bones strewn, stripped with oceanic
proficiency. A gull with wings frozen

mid-flap, the silver arc of a capelin
gripped in its beak. Charcoal guillemots
in cliffside holes, earth-black and curled

in on themselves, like city pigeons.
Amid the curated shambles, a cracked rubber baby
bottle nipple, dry-rot dumbtit,

mottled grey and greenish, nearly
camouflaged against the simulated stones.
Midway down the rock face, puffins

are posed as though about to launch
themselves, in their graceless way,
into the graded blue of the display's back wall,

into the brushstroke line meant to signal horizon.
Above it all, two metallic sprinkler-system
stars shimmer in cool fluorescent light.

Infinity dress

The infinity dress was a lie, and we all bought it.
A circle skirt of quivering, cool silk jersey, two

broad straps plenty long to drape over shoulders,
stretch across breasts, wind around and around

the waist and tie up in a tight, bright bow.
A little something nice to take us

from boardroom to ballroom to bedroom.
One cocoon to metamorphose any woman

into Marilyn on Monday and Farrah on Friday,
Helen on holidays and at the annual regatta,

her face launching a hundred rowboats. A dozen
cunning ways to be the bride's best friend, a dozen

more to stand out or blend. But the joke
was on us: now we know how fifteen

feet of strap gets twisted and twisted
until the dress is not a dress at all, but

just enough rope.

The model train is undergoing repairs

It's out of all proportion: rabbits
like terriers, a mud-coloured
pond with lily pads fixed

in their chase, green-marbled
hole-punch disks with notches
snipped like snapping mouths.

Two ducks stare past a third,
knocked arse-over-kettle, head
and wing resting on the cloudy

surface, unruffled. The steps
to the general store's covered porch
hover, knee-high, impossible,

while a woman in a drop-waist
dress juts her hip, lifts her hand, motions
to no one. The power lines across the dam

have snapped, catgut dragging despite
all signs of hot-glue intervention.
On a piece of ice like a wadded napkin,

two miniature seals recline,
no larger than the seagull lighting
on the teal epoxy harbour.

In the train yard, well-dressed
wives tilt stiff against a car, aquarium-
gravel rubble around their feet.

The mussel hunters

Just half an hour, the narrator explains,
until the tide returns. I watch the hunters
work to pierce an aperture, human-sized,

in the ocean's crumpled mantle. I watch
them as they slip down into the eerie blue
hollow. They are undersea now, but there

is no sea there, just barnacle-spotted stones,
furuncle clustering to carbuncle. The Arctic's
slanting light glows emerald through ancient

sea-ice. Strands of kelp, stems of bladderwrack
hang like streamers, like tossed bouquets caught
in air, spinning out of time. On the ocean

floor, the hunters hunch, plunging bare hands
into seaweed, feeling for this fortune
worth risking their necks for. Their energy

is fervent, keen: they pick till their fingers
plump and prune, salt-crusted, numbing as they
clatter the mussels into aluminum

pails. The treasure glistens onyx, bearded
with broken threads that seconds ago
held creatures to seabed. Against the hush,

a tidal sound returns; the hunters' voices
rise, becoming anxious, a little hinky.
Minutes to escape, emerge, head for some

place solid as the water rushes in
with force enough to animate the groaning
slabs of ice, to float them back up forty feet.

I watch the hunters carry home
their feast, the sky as pink as the soft flesh
waiting in each tight-closed, slick, black shell.

The debt

I have said no to unlit city streets, I have said
no to highways splitting parkland, no
to cuts that make one person do the work
of three. I have said no to shutting schools
and clinics, no to warplanes tracing
ancient paths of caribou, to seabed
bombs that box the ears of whales. I have said
no to filth in rivers.

And, too, I have said yes, I live at this address,
yes, you've spelled my name correctly
on the card, that's it, that's me, yes. Yes
in cabbage-scented parish halls, church
basements, yes in gymnasiums
and auditoriums, yes in libraries, yes
under cold tube lights, over carpeted floors.

We are all debtors here, beholden
to this jagged place for every lungful
of spruce-laced salted air, each slap
of ocean blasting rock and boat, dock
and ankle. Each berry-bucket filled
begs something in return. I pay
my dues with words: a *no* to harm, a *yes*
to harder work. I pay my dues in placards,
ballots, chants, in reckoning.

Single use

> People everywhere are having fun playing—and saying—
> "Roll up the Rim to Win."
>
> —Tim Hortons television commercial, 1995

There is purpose in the gently arcing tower
of stacked cups, purpose in the way the server

spoons heaped measures of white sugar, tips
a doubled quantity of cream, slips

her thumb around the brittle plastic lid, seals
scalding heat inside. There is purpose in the way she fills

a thousand cups, a hundred thousand
cups. She knows just how to stand,

knees soft, white runners planted, the slightest
shift of her body with each reach, each pour, east to west

along the sun's determined path. There is purpose
as customers enter striding, purchase

cups, dream of things they'd like for free
(a bowl of soup, a sports sedan, a new TV)

and when the cups can't make magic happen
there is purpose in the way they're trodden on,

discarded along sidewalks, flattened against
walls, matted in grasses, banking the fenced

rings of schoolyards. There is purpose
in the rain that swells the cups' sides, makes loose

their glued seams, turns paper to fibre to pulp
that storm drains strain through iron teeth, then gulp.

Anniversary

We fell in love, and I had
to get used to a new kind of speaking
in plural. That spring, all the maples
were late with their leaves, or so
it seemed. Grey in May and a risk
of snow. We'd go to work, and
you'd send a dispatch for each patch
of sunlight that appeared in your
office, and I'd do the same
from mine. Thinking of you
thinking of me, of your face turned
to the bright sky for the moment
that it brightened. The moments
of brightness were few, but still
we knew the sun was coming.
This spring, even if it should
come late, we'll measure squares
of sunlight on the floor, and drop
the kids at school and lock
the door. That first night, you held
my hand against your buttoned
shirt and we grinned until our faces
hurt. We stayed that way until the sky
turned light.

Notes

The song lyrics quoted in "Crown," likely misremembered, come from a live performance by the band Thomas Trio and the Red Albino on MuchMusic some time in the early 1990s.

"The water-carriers" is inspired by a photograph by Edith S. Watson and can be seen in *Working the Rock: Newfoundland and Labrador in the Photographs of Edith S. Watson*, 1890-1930 by Frances Rooney (Boulder Books, 2017).

"Barrens" borrows lines from *Romantic Canada* by Victoria Hayward (The Macmillan Company of Canada, 1922).

"Mantel" is written in response to a painting by Kym Greeley; you can see an image of the piece at kymgreeley.com.

"The mussel-hunters" describes a video clip from the 2011 BBC television series *Human Planet*.

Acknowledgements

Versions of poems included here have appeared in *The Walrus*, *Riddle Fence*, *Newfoundland Quarterly*, *Newpoetry.ca*, *Contemporary Verse 2*, *The New Quarterly*, *CBC Poetry Face-Off*, *The Telegram*, and in *The Democracy Cookbook* (edited by Alex Marland and Lisa Moore, ISER Books, 2017). A chapbook edition of "Crown" is available from the lovely people at Anstruther Press.

Creation of *The Debt* was supported by scholarship funding from the Social Sciences and Humanities Research Council (SSHRC) and the School of Graduate Studies at Memorial University.

I am grateful to my editor Luke Hathaway for his faith in these poems, and to my mentor and advisor Mary Dalton for her faith in me. *The Debt* began as a master's thesis at Memorial University; thank you to Jennifer Lokash at Memorial and to Sue Sinclair at University of New Brunswick for their gracious commentary on that project. Thanks, too, to Danine Farquharson for her encouragement, and to Elisabeth de Mariaffi for being the most reasonable person I know. Finally, thank you to Diana Daly for the book's cover image.

Thank you to Bonnie, Charlie, Jude, and Eleanor for not letting me take myself too seriously. And thank you to Mark, always, for everything.

Author photo by Heather Nolan Photography.

Andreae Callanan lives in St. John's with her husband Mark Callanan and their four children. She is a Pierre Elliott Trudeau Foundation scholar and the recipient of the Vanier Canada Scholarship, the F.A. Aldrich Doctoral Fellowship, and, most recently, the Cox & Palmer SPARKS Creative Writing Award. She studies poetry at Memorial University.